Thailand

Sue Townsend

www.heinemann.co.uk/library
Visit our website to find out more information about **Heinemann Library** books.

To order:
☎ Phone 44 (0) 1865 888066
▤ Send a fax to 44 (0) 1865 314091
▭ Visit the Heinemann Bookshop at www.heinemann.co.uk/library to browse our catalogue and order online.

First published in Great Britain by Heinemann Library, Halley Court, Jordan Hill, Oxford OX2 8EJ, a division of Reed Educational and Professional Publishing Ltd. Heinemann is a registered trademark of Reed Educational & Professional Publishing Limited.

OXFORD MELBOURNE AUCKLAND JOHANNESBURG BLANTYRE
GABORONE IBADAN PORTSMOUTH NH (USA) CHICAGO

Designed by Tinstar Design (www.tinstar.co.uk)
Illustrations by Nicholas Beresford-Davies
Originated by Dot Gradations
Printed by Wing King Tong in Hong Kong.

ISBN 0 431 11716 0
06 05 04 03 02
10 9 8 7 6 5 4 3 2 1

British Library Cataloguing in Publication Data
Townsend, Sue
     Thailand. – (A world of recipes)
     1. Cookery, Thai – Juvenile literature
     I. Title
     641.5'123'09593

Acknowledgements
The Publishers would like to thank the following for permission to reproduce photographs:
Corbis: p5. All other photographs: Gareth Boden.

Cover photographs reproduced with permission of Gareth Boden.

Our thanks to Wayne Bailey and Jaikeua Jittiwutikarn for their comments in the preparation of this book.

Every effort has been made to contact copyright holders of any material reproduced in this book. Any omissions will be rectified in subsequent printings if notice is given to the Publisher.

Words appearing in the text in bold, **like this**, are explained in the glossary.

Contents

Key

Key

* easy

** medium

*** difficult

Thai food

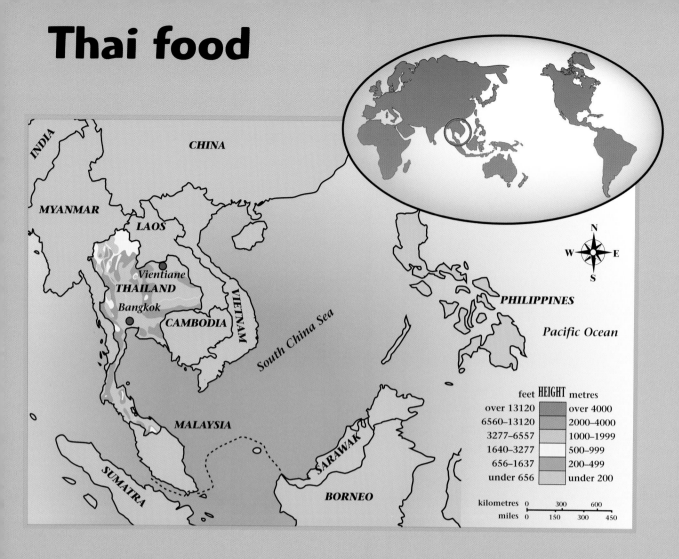

Thailand is part of the Far East. Thai cooking varies from region to region, depending on the land and climate.

In the past

Over 5000 years ago, farmers in Thailand were some of the first people who grew rice for food. Rice is now the most widely-eaten food in the world. The first Thai kingdom was formed in the 13th century, by people who had moved there from China. Today Thailand is a country of great contrasts. If you look across a Thai city you will see large concrete office blocks and beautiful old temples. You can go shopping in modern air-conditioned shops or at a floating market held on boats along the river.

4

Around the country

There are four main regions in Thailand. The north is mountainous. The hottest flavoured dishes come from this region; people here enjoy very spicy foods. In the north-east, the soil is poor and it is very hot, making it difficult to grow crops. The central plains have a **tropical** climate and very **fertile** soil. Rice, vegetables, fruit and herbs grow well. The south has a long coastline, so seafood is plentiful. Farmers here grow rice in **paddy fields**, and have rubber and coconut **plantations**.

Traders in Thailand's floating markets fill their boats with fresh food to sell.

Thai meals

Thai meals consist of several main course dishes served at the same time. When planning a meal, the cook chooses a variety of recipes. These might include a steamed dish, a fried dish, a rice or noodle dish and some vegetables or a salad. There is always a hot-chilli dipping sauce on the table as well. People help themselves to the various dishes and eat with a spoon and fork. Water and tea are traditionally served with meals. Usually fresh fruit is eaten after a main course, but on special occasions, dessert is served before the fruit.

Ingredients

basil

pak choy

ginger

pineapple

sweet chilli sauce

coconut

lemon grass

mange-tout

beansprouts

egg noodles

rice

galangal

mango

garlic

paw paw (papaya)

baby sweetcorn

fine rice noodles

long green beans

chillies

Beansprouts

Beansprouts are grown from mung beans. They are used in stir-fries and salads. Most supermarkets sell them. Make sure you buy fresh, crisp-looking beansprouts.

Coconut

Coconut is a popular ingredient in Thai cooking. It adds a creamy flavour to recipes. It can be used as coconut milk, which you buy in cans or as creamed coconut, which comes in hard blocks.

Fish sauce

Thai cooks use this salty sauce to add a special flavour to recipes. They call it *nam pla*. You can buy it in bottles from most large supermarkets.

Herbs

The main herbs used in Thai cooking are basil and coriander. Holy basil is the most popular, with its hot flavour. You can use European basil and a little chopped chilli instead. Coriander has a fresh, strong flavour.

Palm sugar

Palm sugar is made from the sap of coconut trees. It has a strong flavour. It is difficult to buy outside Thailand, but you can use dark muscovado or soft brown sugar instead.

Spices

Spices are plants or seeds with strong flavours. Some of the common ones in Thai cooking are the roots **galangal** and ginger. Lemon grass has a strong lemony flavour. **Tamarind** has a sweet-sour taste and it is easiest to buy as a paste. (If you can't find tamarind, use lime or lemon juice instead.) Chillies come in a variety of sizes and some are hotter than others. If you don't like hot flavours, leave the chillies out. Always remove the seeds, and wash your hands well after preparing chillies.

Tofu

Tofu is made from soya beans that have been **mashed** into a pulp. It is sold in small blocks from chilled food cabinets or in foil-wrapped packages.

Rice

Thai cooks use three main types of rice – Jasmine rice (or Thai fragrant rice) has long grains, glutinous rice has short grains and becomes sticky when cooked and black glutinous rice is dark brown.

Rice vinegar

Rice vinegar is clear with no colour.

Before you start

Kitchen rules

There are a few basic rules you should always follow when you are cooking:

- Ask an adult if you can use the kitchen.
- Some cooking processes, especially those involving hot water or oil can be dangerous. When you see this sign, take extra care and ask an adult for help.
- Wash your hands before you start.
- Wear an apron to protect your clothes. Tie back long hair.
- Be very careful when you use sharp knives.
- Never leave pan handles sticking out in case you knock them.
- Always use oven gloves to lift things in and out of the oven.
- Wash fruit and vegetables before you use them.
- Always wash chopping boards and work surfaces very well after use, especially after chopping raw meat, fish or poultry.

How long will it take?

Some of the recipes in this book are quick and easy, and some are more difficult and take longer. The strip across the top of the right hand page of each recipe tells you how long it will take you to prepare each dish from start to finish. It also shows how difficult each dish is to make: every recipe is
* (easy), ** (medium) or *** (difficult).

Quantities and measurements

You can see how many people each recipe will serve at the top of each right hand page. You can multiply or divide the quantities if you want to cook for more or fewer people.

Ingredients for recipes can be measured in two ways. Metric measurements use grams and millilitres. Imperial measurements use ounces and fluid ounces. This book uses metric measurements. If you want to convert these into imperial measurements, see the chart on page 44.

In the recipes you will see the following abbreviations:

tbsp = tablespoon   g = grams   cm = centimetre
tsp = teaspoon   ml = millilitres

Utensils

To cook the recipes in this book, you will need these utensils (as well as essentials, such as spoons, plates and bowls):

- chopping board
- wok
- metal steamer
- food processor
  or blender
- electric whisk
- large frying pan
- grater
- measuring spoons
- small screw-topped jar
- saucepans with lids
  (non-stick)
- set of scales
- sharp knife
- lemon juicer
- wooden skewers
- colander

 Whenever you use kitchen knives, be very careful.

Satay

In Thailand, satay is often cooked and sold on street stalls. You can either choose to make satay from beef or chicken, but you must **marinate**, cook and serve the beef and chicken separately. Serve satay as a starter.

What you need

2cm piece fresh ginger
2 tsp ground cumin
1 tsp magic paste (see page 11)
2 tsp fish sauce
2 tsp sweet chilli sauce (see page 33)
3 tbsp creamed coconut
2 cloves garlic
juice of ½ a lemon or lime
450g boneless, skinless chicken breast

For the sauce:
6 tbsp crunchy peanut butter
1½ tbsp creamed coconut
8 tbsp cold water
fresh coriander leaves
wedges of lemon or lime for squeezing over satay

What you do

1 **Peel** and **grate** the ginger. Stir the cumin, magic paste, fish sauce, ginger and sweet chilli sauce together in a large bowl.

2 Finely grate the creamed coconut and stir into the spice mixture. Peel and finely **chop** or crush the garlic. Stir the lime or lemon juice and garlic into the mixture.

3 Cut the chicken breasts into 2cm cubes. Stir them into the spice mixture. **Cover** and **chill** in the fridge for at least one hour or overnight.

4 Soak 6–8 wooden **skewers** in water for 20 minutes to help stop them burning.

(!) 5 Push the chicken onto the skewers and **grill** for 12 minutes. Turn the skewers frequently until the meat is cooked. Test by cutting one piece of meat in half – the flesh should be white with no sign of pink.

6 Put the peanut butter, creamed coconut and 8 tablespoons cold water into a non-stick saucepan. Heat gently, stirring all the time.

7 Spoon the sauce into a dish and serve with the chicken. **Garnish** with fresh coriander and wedges of lemon or lime.

MAGIC PASTE

Magic paste is a ready-mixed blend of garlic, ginger and coriander root. You can find it in jars in a large supermarket. If you don't have any, use a little grated ginger, chopped fresh coriander and extra garlic.

Rice pancakes with prawns and stir-fried vegetables

In Thailand, cooks make rice pancakes at home using rice flour and water. Large supermarkets or oriental food shops sell ready-made pancakes.

What you need

1 carrot
1 spring onion
2 tsp vegetable oil
16 large cooked, peeled prawns (**thawed** in fridge overnight if using frozen prawns)
50g bean sprouts
1 tsp sweet chilli sauce
50g packet rice flour pancakes (contains 8 pancakes)

What you do

1 **Peel** and **slice** the carrot into matchstick-size strips.

2 Cut the top and bottom off the spring onion. **Slice** it into thin strips.

(!) 3 Heat the oil in a wok or frying pan. **Stir-fry** the carrot and spring onion for 2 minutes. Add the prawns and bean sprouts and stir-fry for 1 minute. Stir in the sweet chilli sauce and leave to cool.

4 Put 6 tbsps of water onto a plate. Dip a pancake in. Leave for 1 minute or until soft.

5 Lay the pancake out flat on a baking tray or chopping board.

6 Put two prawns into the centre of the pancake and top with a little of the vegetables.

7 Fold over one side of the pancake into the centre. Fold in the sides and then roll up with the join underneath.

8 Repeat this until you have made eight pancake rolls.

9 Carefully, poke holes in greaseproof paper with a **skewer**. Line the bottom of a steamer with the paper and lay the pancakes on it.

(!) 10 Put the steamer over a pan filled with hot water and bring to the **boil**. **Cover** and cook for 5 minutes.

11 Serve the pancakes as a starter with sweet chilli dipping sauce if you like it (see page 33).

Chicken and noodle soup

Soup is not served as a starter in Thailand, but as part of a main meal. Bowls of soup are put onto the table with the other main course dishes. People help themselves to all the dishes.

What you need

¼ red chilli (if you like it)
1 small boneless,
  skinless chicken breast
1 clove garlic
1 tbsp oil
1 tsp ground cumin
1 chicken stock cube
25g pak choy or
  Chinese leaf
few sprigs fresh coriander
25g fine rice noodles
25g bean sprouts

What you do

1 Cut out the seeds of the chilli and finely **chop** it. Wash your hands very well afterwards.

2 Cut the chicken breast into long thin strips.

3 **Peel** and finely **chop** the garlic. Heat the oil in a large saucepan and gently heat the cumin for 30 seconds. Add the garlic and stir for 30 seconds.

4 Add the chicken and chilli to the pan. Carefully add 450ml of cold water to the pan. It may spit a bit as the pan is hot.

5 Crumble the stock cube and stir it into the saucepan. Bring to the **boil**, **cover** and **simmer** for 15 minutes.

6 **Slice** the pak choy into thin strips. Chop the coriander.

7 Add the fine rice noodles to the pan and boil for 4 minutes.

8 Add the pak choy or Chinese leaf, coriander and bean sprouts to the soup.

9 Bring to the boil and serve immediately. Warn everyone that the soup will be very hot.

Stir-fried noodles with pork, chicken, prawns and vegetables

What you need

175g pork **tenderloin**
1 boneless, skinless
  chicken breast
juice of 1 lime
3 tbsp fish sauce
2 tbsp palm sugar or
  soft brown sugar
2 cloves garlic
½ a red chilli (if you like it)
1 red pepper
4 spring onions
75g pak choy or Chinese leaf
225g pack egg thread noodles
4 tbsp vegetable oil
150g cooked, peeled prawns
50g peanuts
2 eggs

In Thailand, people use chopsticks to eat dishes with noodles in them. This recipe mixes meat, poultry and seafood, which is common in Thai cooking.

What you do

1 Cut the pork and chicken into thin strips.

2 Stir the lime juice, fish sauce and sugar together.

3 **Peel** and crush or **chop** the garlic.

4 Remove the seeds from the chilli and pepper. Finely chop the chilli and **slice** the pepper. Wash your hands well after handling the chilli.

5 Slice the tops and ends off the spring onions. Cut the stems into 5cm pieces and then into very fine strips.

6 Cut the pak choy or Chinese leaf into 5cm squares.

7 Put the noodles into a pan of boiling water, cover and **simmer** for 5 minutes, until they are soft.

(!) **8** Heat the oil in a wok or frying pan. Add the garlic and chilli, then the pork and chicken. **Stir-fry** for 3 minutes. Add the prawns, pepper and spring onion, and stir-fry for 2 minutes.

9 **Drain** the noodles and add them to the pan. Stir the lime juice mixture and add it to the pan with the pak choy or Chinese leaf and peanuts.

10 **Beat** the eggs and pour them in. Stir-fry until the eggs have set. Serve immediately.

Fish with spring onion, ginger and carrot

In Thailand, cooks take the insides out of fish like pomfret or bream and fill them with vegetables and spices. Supermarkets here sell ready-filleted fish, which is easier to use. Look for red snapper or sea bass fillets, or use cod or salmon instead.

What you need

1 carrot
3 spring onions
5cm piece ginger
1 tsp rice vinegar
1 tsp vegetable oil
2 x 200g fish fillets,
   (preferably with
   skin on)

What you do

1 Preheat oven to 180°C/ 350°F/gas mark 4. **Peel** the carrot and **slice** it into matchstick-size strips.

2 Trim the tops and ends off the spring onions and slice into long thin strips.

3 Using a vegetable peeler, peel the skin off the ginger and finely **grate** the pale-coloured root.

4 Put the ginger and any juice from it, the carrot and spring onion into a bowl. Sprinkle the rice vinegar over them.

5 Put a large piece of foil onto a baking tray. Brush the foil with a little oil. Put a fillet of fish, skin side down, onto the foil.

6 Spoon the vegetables over the fish and lay the rest around it. Place the other fillet on top, skin side up.

7 Bring the sides of the foil up. Pinch the edges together to seal it into a parcel.

⊘ **8** **Bake** for 20–25 minutes until the fish feels firm to the touch. Be careful of the hot steam as you open the parcel. Using a fish slice, lift the fish out of the foil onto a dish.

9 Arrange the vegetables around the fish. Serve with rice (see page 27) or noodles (see page 17) and chilli dipping sauce if you like spicy food (see page 33).

Stir-fried vegetables with lemon grass and galangal

If you cannot find the spicy root **galangal**, you can replace it with an equal amount of ginger and 1 tbsp of lemon juice. Thai meals always include a vegetable or salad dish.

What you need

3 spring onions
1 carrot
100g mange tout
100g pak choy or Chinese leaf
5cm piece of galangal root
2 sticks lemon grass
2 tbsp vegetable oil
200g baby sweetcorn
50g bean sprouts

What you do

1 Cut the tops and bottoms off the spring onions.

2 **Peel** the carrot.

3 **Slice** the carrot and spring onions into thin strips about 5cm long.

4 Trim the tips from the mange tout.

5 Cut the pak choy or Chinese leaf into 5cm squares.

6 Peel and finely **grate** the **galangal**.

7 Cut the bottom and outer leaf from the lemon grass. Slice the stem into very thin rounds.

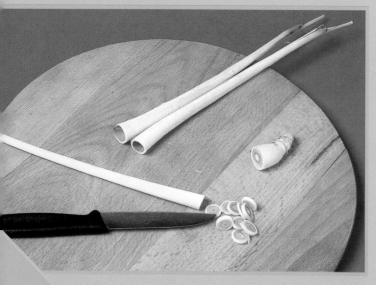

8 Heat the oil in a wok or large frying pan. Add the lemon grass and **galangal**. Let it sizzle for 1 minute, then add the spring onions and carrots. **Stir-fry** for 1 minute.

9 Add the mange tout and baby sweetcorn to the pan. Stir-fry for 2 minutes.

10 Add the pak choy or Chinese leaf and bean sprouts. Stir-fry for 2 minutes. Serve with noodles, or with a main meal dish like chicken with basil (page 24), or chilli pineapple rice (page 26).

Long green beans with coconut

Cooking with coconut milk is very popular in southern Thailand, where farmers grow coconuts. If you cannot find long beans, use French beans instead. Cook them in a non-stick pan, so that the coconut milk will not burn.

What you need

300g long green beans
   or French beans
300ml coconut milk

What you do

1 Cut the ends off the beans and **slice** them into 5cm-long pieces.

2 Put the beans into a non-stick pan and cover with water. Bring to the **boil** and **simmer** for 1 minute.

(!) **3** Carefully **drain** the beans through a colander.

4 Put the beans back into the saucepan and pour the coconut milk over them.

5 Heat gently and simmer for 2 minutes. Serve hot.

DINING THAI STYLE

A main course in Thailand is made up of three to four different dishes to which you help yourself. For a special meal, people serve six to eight dishes. This might include **stir-fried** vegetables with lemon grass and **galangal** (see page 20); long green beans with coconut; chicken with basil (see page 24); chilli pineapple rice (see page 26) and crab and spring onion cakes (see page 30). The main meal might end with a dessert or fruit.

Chicken with basil

This dish is often **garnished** with basil. In Thailand, cooks may **deep-fry** basil to give it a crisp texture. Street traders cooking food often make and sell this dish.

What you need

4 boneless, skinless chicken breasts
3 tbsp fish sauce
2 tsp soy sauce
1 tsp caster sugar
1 red chilli (if you like it)
4 cloves garlic
2 tbsp vegetable oil
10–12 Thai or European basil leaves

What you do

1 Cut the chicken into 2cm pieces.

2 Stir the fish sauce, soy sauce and sugar together.

3 Scrape out the seeds from the chilli and throw them away. Finely **chop** the chilli. Wash your hands well afterwards.

4 **Peel** and finely **slice** the garlic.

5 Heat the oil in a wok or large frying pan. Add the garlic and chilli and **stir-fry** for 1 minute. Add the chicken and stir-fry for 5 minutes.

6 Pour in the fish sauce mixture and cook for another 3 minutes.

7 Add the basil leaves and serve immediately. Garnish with a spring onion tassel if you like (see box below).

HOW TO MAKE SPRING ONION TASSELS

Cut the bottoms and tops from two spring onions. Make lengthways cuts from either end of the stems, leaving the centre uncut so that each end looks like a tassel.

Leave the spring onions in a bowl of cold water for 10 minutes to make their ends curl. Shake off any water and use your tassels to garnish a dish.

Chilli pineapple rice

This dish looks stunning served in a hollowed out pineapple shell, but you could just put it into a bowl if you prefer. This recipe is from northern Thailand where hot, sweet and sour dishes are very popular.

What you need

200g Jasmine or
   long grain rice
1 chilli (if you like it)
½ red pepper
2 spring onions
1 tbsp fish sauce
1 tbsp soy sauce
100g fresh pineapple

What you do

1 Cook the rice (see page 27, opposite).

2 Scoop out the seeds from the chilli and pepper and throw them away. Finely **chop** the chilli and **slice** the pepper. Wash your hands well afterwards.

3 Cut the tops and bottoms off the spring onions. Slice the stems into thin rings.

4 Stir the chilli, pepper, onions, fish sauce and soy sauce together.

5 Carefully cut the pineapple in half along its length and through the leaves. Using a small knife, cut all the way around just inside the skin to loosen the flesh.

6 Cut down the sides of the tough core in the middle of the pineapple. Ease out the fruit either side of the core. Cut out the flesh under the core. Throw away the core. Weigh 100g of fruit and finely chop it. (You can use the remaining pineapple in another recipe or eat it as dessert.)

7 When the rice is cooked, stir the pineapple and chilli mixture into it. Spoon the rice mixture into the pineapple shell and serve hot with fish, chicken or meat dishes.

TO COOK RICE

Bring plenty of water to **boil** in a large pan. Add salt. When the water is boiling, add the rice. Bring the pan back to the **boil**, stir well and cover. **Simmer** for 15 minutes. **Drain** the rice into a large sieve or colander.

Paw paw salad

Thai cooks often carve fruit and vegetables into decorative shapes. They use them to **garnish** dishes. Paw paws (also called papayas) are perfect for this, because of their rich red-orange colour.

What you need

For the salad:
2 paw paws (papayas)
½ a cucumber
2 spring onions
50g bean sprouts

For the dressing:
3 tbsp vegetable oil
1 tsp fish sauce
2 tbsp lime or
    lemon juice
1 tsp palm sugar or
    dark muscovado sugar
¼ red or green
    chilli (if you like it)

What you do

1 To make the **dressing** put the oil, fish sauce, lime or lemon juice and sugar into a screw-topped jar.

2 Cut open the chilli and throw away the seeds. Finely **chop** it and add to the dressing. Wash your hands well.

3 Cut the paw paws in half. Using a teaspoon, scoop out the seeds and throw them away.

4 **Peel** off the paw paw skins. **Slice** the fruits thinly crossways (see the slices on page 29).

5 Peel the cucumber and cut in half lengthways. Scoop out the watery centre with a teaspoon and throw it away. Thinly slice the cucumber.

6 Cut the bottoms and tops off the spring onions. Finely slice them into rings.

7 Arrange the paw paw, cucumber, spring onions and bean sprouts on a plate.

8 Put the lid on the jar and shake the dressing well. Spoon it over the salad just before serving. Serve as a side dish with chicken with basil (page 24) or crab and spring onion cakes (page 30).

Crab and spring onion cakes

In Thailand, it is traditional to offer food to Buddhist monks, who rely on these gifts to survive. Monks travel along the rivers collecting food from families who live on the river banks. Thai recipes often contain fish because it is so readily available.

What you need

2 x 170g cans
   white crabmeat
3 spring onions
3 tbsp fresh coriander
1 egg
2 tsp cornflour
2 tbsp vegetable oil
sprigs of fresh coriander

What you do

1 Tip the crabmeat into a large sieve. Press the crab with the back of a spoon to squeeze out the liquid. Then put the meat in a bowl.

2 Cut the bottoms and tops off the spring onions. Finely **slice** them into rings. **Chop** the coriander.

3 Crack the egg over a bowl. Pass the yolk between the two shell halves so all the white drips into the bowl. Lightly **beat** the egg white with a fork.

4 Stir the spring onion, coriander, egg white and cornflour into the crab and mix well.

5 Put a 7.5cm round pastry cutter on a plate. Fill it with 3 tbsp of crab mixture and press with the back of a spoon. Lift the cutter off. Repeat this to make eight crab cakes. (If you prefer, you can shape the cakes with your hands.)

(!) 6 Heat the oil in a frying pan. **Fry** the crab cakes over a medium heat for 4 minutes or until lightly browned. Using a fish slice, turn the cakes over and cook for a further 4 minutes.

7 Lift the cakes out of the pan and place on a serving dish.

8 Decorate the crab cakes with sprigs of coriander. Serve hot as part of a Thai meal, perhaps with chilli pineapple rice (see page 26) and paw paw salad (see page 28). They also make a delicious snack with some chilli dipping sauce (see page 33).

Rice, prawns and tofu

Rice is eaten at least once a day by Thais and is their **staple** food. This makes a tasty **vegetarian** dish if you leave out the prawns. When the **paddy fields** around a village are being planted with new rice seedlings, all the villagers go to help the farmers.

What you need

200g long grain rice
250g packet tofu
    (beancurd)
3 spring onions
2 tbsp oil
2 tbsp **tamarind** paste
200g large cooked,
    peeled prawns
2 tbsp fish sauce
1 tsp caster sugar

What you do

1 Cook the rice (see page 27).

2 Cut the tofu into 2cm cubes.

3 Cut the bottoms and tops off the spring onions. **Slice** the stems into thin rings.

(!) 4 Heat the oil in a wok or large frying pan. **Stir-fry** the spring onions for 1 minute.

5 Add the **tamarind** paste, tofu, prawns, fish sauce and sugar. Stir-fry for 3 minutes.

6 Add the cooked rice to the pan and stir well. Serve this with a sweet chilli dipping sauce (see box below).

SWEET CHILLI SAUCE

Sweet chilli sauce is often served with meals for dipping food into. It adds a hot, spicy flavour. Sweet chilli sauce is also added to dishes as a quick way to create a spicy taste. Serve it with the **savoury** dishes in this book if you like chilli in your food!

Coconut tapioca with mango

Thai desserts are very sweet. They are served after a main meal on special occasions. To finish the meal, people eat fresh fruit. Tapioca is small 'beads' made from cassava flour. They soak up the coconut milk and become fatter as they cook.

What you need

50g pearl tapioca
400ml coconut milk
2 tbsp caster sugar
1 mango

What you do

1 Put the tapioca in a non-stick saucepan with the coconut milk and 400ml water. Cook on a medium heat, stirring all the time, until the coconut milk starts to bubble.

2 **Cover** the pan. Turn the heat down and **simmer** for 30 minutes, stirring every 5 minutes.

3 Mix in the sugar and take the pan off the heat. Allow to cool, then **chill** in the fridge for about 2 hours.

4 Cut the mango lengthways into three equal pieces. The middle section will contain the large, flat stone. Cut off the skin and **slice** the fruit into long strips. Trim any fruit away from the stone.

5 Stir the tapioca and divide it between four bowls. Arrange the mango slices on top.

COCONUT

Coconuts are used in several different forms. Coconut milk is made from water mixed with the grated white flesh. Creamed coconut looks like a block of white butter and needs to be **grated** and measured before it can be added to recipes. Sometimes, desiccated and shredded coconut are used in cooking. Desiccated coconut is grated coconut that has been dried. Shredded coconut is still moist and is usually sweetened.

Coconut and mango ice cream

Ice cream is not a traditional Thai food, but it is very popular in such a hot country. People sell plain and fruit-flavoured ice creams in the street. In Thailand, ice cream is often served in paper cups rather than in wafer cones.

What you need

6 tbsp creamed
  coconut
600ml milk
5 eggs
1 tbsp cornflour
75g caster sugar
1 large mango (or 2
  small mangoes)
600ml double cream

What you do

1 **Grate** the creamed coconut, then measure out 6 tbsp of it.

2 Put the milk into a saucepan and heat until **simmering**.

3 With a fork, **beat** the eggs and cornflour together.

4 Carefully **whisk** the hot milk into the eggs. Pour this mixture back into the pan. Cook on a low heat, stirring until it has thickened. Mix in the sugar.

5 Divide the mixture between two bowls. Stir the grated coconut into one bowl.

6 Cut two circles of greaseproof paper. Dampen them and place one on top of each bowl to stop a skin from forming. Leave to cool.

7 Slice the mango lengthways into three pieces. Cut off the skin and slice the fruit. Trim the fruit around the stone.

8 Put the mango into a food processor and process until smooth. Mix it into the bowl of plain mixture.

9 Using an electric or hand whisk, whisk the cream until it is firm enough to form soft peaks. Stir half into the coconut mixture and half into the mango mixture.

10 Pour each mixture into a freezer-proof plastic box. Freeze for 1 hour, then whisk with an electric or hand whisk. Freeze for another hour and whisk. Freeze overnight.

11 Move the ice cream into the fridge 30 minutes before you want to serve it. If you like, decorate it with mango slices and coconut shavings.

COCONUT SHAVINGS

Ask an adult to help you break open a fresh coconut. Loosen the white flesh from the coconut shell. With a potato peeler, shave off thin strips of coconut.

Fried bananas

In Thailand, people can buy bananas from boats in the floating markets along the rivers. When you buy bananas, make sure they are firm, with skin that is still a bit green. In Thailand, bananas and coconut are often cooked together. Bananas are served cooked in coconut milk or coated in dried coconut, as in this recipe.

What you need

1 thick slice white bread
75g shredded coconut
2 eggs
2 tbsp plain flour
4 firm bananas
4 tbsp vegetable oil
juice of 1 lime
slices of lime

What you do

1 Trim the crusts off the bread. Cut the slice into small pieces and put in a blender or food processor. Process the bread to make it into breadcrumbs.

2 Mix the crumbs and the coconut on a large plate.

3 **Beat** the eggs lightly and pour them on to a plate.

4 Put the flour in a plastic bag. Peel the bananas and, one at a time, put them into the bag of flour. Shake the bag gently to **coat** them.

5 Dip the bananas into the egg, coating them completely. Now roll each banana in the coconut crumbs.

Ready to eat: 20 minutes, difficulty: ✱✱, serves 4

6 With adult help, heat the oil in a large frying pan. Add the bananas and fry gently on both sides, until golden.

7 Put the bananas on a plate. Squeeze the lime juice over them. Decorate with lime slices if you like, and serve them warm.

BANANA SNACKS

In Thailand, bananas are quite small. Children enjoy dipping them into a sweet, sticky plum sauce, then into grated coconut or toasted sesame seeds. Bananas are also flattened with a small wooden board, covered with a little honey then dried in the sun to make a chewy snack.

Fresh fruit platter

All over Thailand you will see platefuls of beautifully sliced fruits and fresh flowers left out in the open. These are prepared by Thai people as offerings to their **Buddhist** gods.

What you need

1 mango
1 paw paw (papaya)
1 small pineapple
200g fresh lychees
   (or canned if you
   cannot find fresh
   lychees)

What you do

1 Cut the mango lengthways into three equal pieces, the middle section will contain the large, flat stone. Cut off the skin and **slice** the fruit into long strips. Trim any fruit away from the stone.

2 Cut the paw paw in half. Using a teaspoon, scoop out the seeds. With a vegetable peeler, **peel** off the paw paw skin. Cut the fruit crossways into thin slices.

3 Cut the pineapple in half lengthways, then trim off the leaves. Slide a small knife between the fruit and the skin and cut all the way around.

(!) 4 Cut down either side of the core in the middle of the pineapple. Ease out the fruit sections from either side of the core and slice them. Cut away the fruit under the core and slice that as well. Throw away the core and the skin.

5 Using a sharp knife or your thumbnail, lift a little of the skin off the lychees, then peel them completely. Cut them in half to remove the stone.

6 Arrange all the fruits on a large plate. Serve them slightly **chilled**.

Refreshing fruit cocktail

Smart hotels in Bangkok, the capital of Thailand, serve juice-filled pineapples, coconuts and paw paws (papayas) decorated with slices of fruit and mini parasols. In Thai homes, drinks are only served like this for special occasions.

What you need

2 paw paws (papayas)
100ml pineapple juice
100ml orange juice
1 lime
2 straws

To decorate:
2 mini parasols
   (optional)
pieces of fresh fruit

What you do

1 Carefully cut a very thin **slice** off the bottom of a paw paw, so that it will stand up.

2 Make a 5cm cut into the top of the paw paw, as if you were about to cut it in half. Cut across from the side, 5cm from the top, towards the centre. This will cut out a section of the paw paw.

3 Using a teaspoon, scoop out the seeds and throw away.

4 Scrape out some of the fruit and put into a blender. Leave enough of the flesh around the sides so that the paw paw will not leak when filled with fruit juice. Do the same with the second paw paw.

5 Blend the fruit in a blender until smooth. Add the pineapple and orange juice. Squeeze the juice from the lime and add to the mixture. Blend again and pour the mixture into a jug.

6 Carefully pour the juice into the paw paws. Place each fruit on a saucer and add straws. Decorate with parasols and fresh fruit if you want to.

Further information

Here are some places to find out more about Thai cooking.

Books

Children's World Cookbook
Usborne

Hamlyn Essential Thai: Step-by-step Recipes with Style
Hamlyn, 1997.

Websites

www.asiafood.org
www.gezi.com/gzworld/recipe/index.html
www.recipesource.com/ethnic/asia/thai/

Conversion chart

Ingredients for recipes can be measured in two different ways. Metric measurements use grams and millilitres. Imperial measurements use ounces and fluid ounces. This book uses metric measurements. The chart here shows you how to convert measurements from metric to imperial.

SOLIDS		LIQUIDS	
METRIC	IMPERIAL	METRIC	IMPERIAL
10g	¼ oz	30ml	1 fl oz
15g	½ oz	50ml	2 fl oz
25g	1 oz	75ml	2½ fl oz
50g	1¾ oz	100ml	3½ fl oz
75g	2¾ oz	125ml	4 fl oz
100g	3½ oz	150ml	5 fl oz
150g	5 oz	300ml	10 fl oz
250g	9 oz	600ml	20 fl oz
450g	16 oz	1litre	30½ fl oz

Healthy eating

This diagram shows you which foods you should eat to stay healthy. Most of your food should come from the bottom of the pyramid. Eat some of the foods from the middle every day. Only eat a little of the foods from the top.

Healthy eating Thai style

In Thailand, rice is an important part of people's diet and as you can see belongs in the bottom layer of the pyramid. Thai recipes also use lots of fruit and vegetables as they grow so plentifully. The small amounts of meat that Thai people eat are not fatty. Chicken and fish are usually cooked by **stir-frying** in a wok so only small amounts of oil are added.

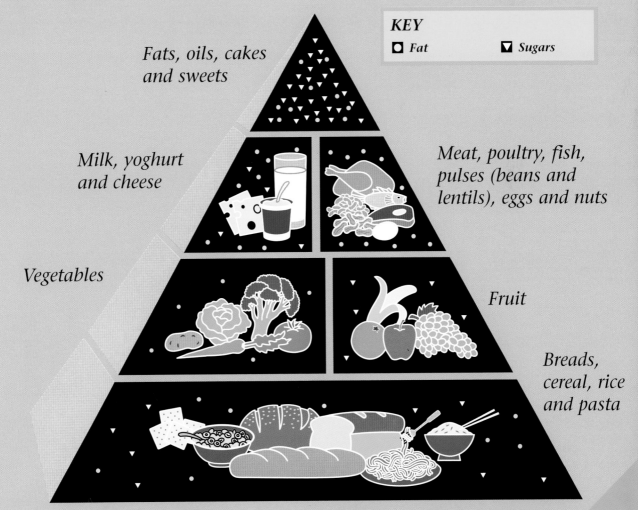

Fats, oils, cakes and sweets

KEY
◻ Fat   ▼ Sugars

Milk, yoghurt and cheese

Meat, poultry, fish, pulses (beans and lentils), eggs and nuts

Vegetables

Fruit

Breads, cereal, rice and pasta

Glossary

bake cook something in the oven

beat mix ingredients together strongly, using a fork or whisk

boil cook a liquid on the hob. Boiling liquid bubbles and steams strongly.

Buddhist somebody who follows the Buddhist religion

chill put a dish in the fridge for a while before serving

chop cut into pieces using a sharp knife

coat cover with a mixture or sauce

cover put a lid on a pan, or put foil or cling film over a dish

deep-fry cook in a deep pan of hot oil

drain remove liquid, usually by pouring something into colander or sieve

dressing sauce for a salad

fertile good for growing things in

galangal root that tastes like lemon and ginger

garnish decorate food, for example, with fresh herbs

grate break something, for example cheese, into small pieces using a grater

grill cook under a grill

marinate soak food, especially meat or fish, in a liquid to add flavour

mash crush a food until it is soft and pulpy

monk a man who has dedicated his life to religion

paddy field field that is flooded, making it suitable for growing rice

peel remove the skin of a fruit or vegetable

plantations big farms that grow crops such as rubber and rice

savoury the opposite of sweet. Savoury dishes may contain meat, fish, eggs or cheese.

simmer cook liquid on the hob. Simmering liquid bubbles and steams gently.

slice cut ingredients into thin flat pieces

staple ingredient that is eaten often by the population of a country

stir-fry cook foods in a little oil over a high heat, stirring all of the time

tamarind a fruit with a brown pod containing a sweet-sour pulp used for cooking

tenderloin lean cut of meat, usually pork

thawed frozen item that has been defrosted

tropical hot, wet climate

vegetarian food that does not contain meat. People who don't eat meat are called vegetarians.

whisk mix ingredients using a whisk

Index

Titles in the *World of Recipes* series include:

Hardback   0 431 11714 4

Hardback   0 431 11717 9

Hardback   0 431 11715 2

Hardback   0 431 11716 0

Find out about the other titles in this series on our website www.heinemann.co.uk/library